How to Handle Your MUM

By Roy Apps

Illustrated by Nick Sharratt

Contents

How to Handle Your MUM

By Roy Apps

Illustrated by Nick Sharratt

This edition first published in 2014
by Franklin Watts

Text © Roy Apps 2014
Illustration* © Nick Sharratt 2014
Cover design by Cathryn Gilbert
Layouts by Blue Paw Design

Franklin Watts
338 Euston Road
London NW1 3BH

Th... author and illustrator have...
accord... ...38.

A CIP catalogue record for this book
is available from the British Library.

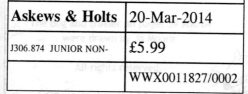

(pb) ISBN: 978 1 4451 2393 6
(ebook) ISBN: 978 1 4451 2397 4
(Library ebook) ISBN: 978 1 4451 2401 8

1 3 5 7 9 10 8 6 4 2

Printed in Great Britain

Franklin Watts is a division of Hachette Children's Books,
an Hachette UK company.
www.hachette.co.uk

Warning!

The information contained in this book can be highly dangerous if it falls into the wrong hands, i.e. your mum's.

To prevent this from happening you should take one of the following precautions:

1. Memorise every word in the book and then eat it.*

2. If you are a girl, disguise the nature of this book by slipping it inside a copy of your algebra homework folder — Mum will never look in there.

3. If you are a boy, hide this book in your gym bag — Mum will never look in there.

* TV chef Jammy Owl-Liver suggests you try the following recipe if you do decide to eat this book. Extra Whopper Book Burger (i) Place book in a stale sesame seed bun. (ii) Place book-filled bun on a plate. (iii) Add two tablespoons of extra hot chillies. (iv) Eat (the bun, not the napkin).

How To Handle Your Mum:

Stage One

Why it's important to be able to handle your mum — NOW!

Ask yourself this question:

What's the difference between your mum and a mountain bike with square wheels and 57 reverse gears?

Tricky one, this, so here's a picture to help you.

Did you see the gears on that bike? What a laugh! Now look at the gear on that mum — what an even bigger laugh! But to get back to the question: the difference between your mum and a mountain bike with square wheels and 57 reverse gears is that you can't take your mum back to the shop!
If you could, it would be dead easy to find a model that was easy to handle. No. You've got to learn to handle the mum you've got.

We regret mums cannot be exchanged

It's important to be able to handle your mum now, because the older you get, the more difficult it becomes. In fact, the only people who don't need to learn how to handle their mums are newborn babies. They've got it (or rather her) completely and absolutely worked out. Take the following scenes. Done that? Now put them back in the book and read them!

Scene 1

YOU: (Slamming the front door behind you and yelling at the top of your voice) Hey, Mum! Mum!!! I wanna Coke!

YOUR MUM: Come back in again like a civilised human being, speak properly and remember the magic word...

YOU: (Coming in again, this time closing the door quietly and speaking in hushed tones) Mum? Could I have a Coke, please?

YOUR MUM: No, you can't. We're just about to have dinner.

(Result: You don't get your Coke.)

Scene 2

NEWBORN BABY: (Hammering fists on Mum's chest)

Wahhh!!!
Waaahh!

MUM: Ooo…my little darling. Do you want a drink? (Result: baby gets a drink.)

Scene 3

It is half past nine in the morning. You are lying down on your bed, taking a well earned, post-breakfast rest, kind of half-dozing, half-daydreaming about how much better your life will be when you finally become a World-Beating Number One Sports Superstar. Suddenly a tornado blasts into the room. It's…

YOUR MUM: Oh, for goodness' sake, (insert your name here)! Get up, you great schlummock and go and do something useful like learning to play the clarinet or hoovering your room or visiting your grandmother. (Result: either you learn to play the clarinet, tidy up your room and visit your grandmother, or you reach a compromise and learn how to hoover up your grandmother with a clarinet.)

WOOSH!

Scene 4

It is half past nine in the morning. The newborn baby is lying down in its cot, taking a well-earned rest, half-dozing, half-daydreaming under his Kipper the dog mobile. Suddenly a kind and gentle breeze wafts into the room. It is —

MUM: Aaahhhh... Does my little darling want to go to sleepy-byes?

(Sings) Bye, Baby Bunting, etc., etc.

(Result: baby is left on his own to do whatever he wants until it's time for another drink. [See Scene 2.])

So there you have it. Either you can go back to being a baby again and start wearing stinky nappies, or you can read this book. Which method do you fancy? Tricky decision, eh? You probably need two seconds to decide. So here they are:

ONE SECOND
ANOTHER SECOND

Made your choice? OK, for those of you who have decided to become babies again, I hope you'll have a nappy time! Don't forget you'll need a dummy too.

On second thoughts, you won't need a dummy, because you probably are one.

For those incredibly intelligent and sensible people who have decided to learn how to handle their mums by reading this brilliant book, the first thing you must do is this:

Keep reading!

The second thing you must do is:

Turn over!

How To Handle Your Mum:

Stage Two

Finding out just what kind of mum you've got

Just what kind of mum have you got? There's a very simple answer to this, which is — how on earth do you expect me to know? You've never even introduced me to her.

There are only three kinds of mum who are easy to cope with, and there aren't many of them left. These mums are rather like mountain gorillas and leatherback turtles. They are an endangered species!

TYPE 1: The Mummy-Type Mum

An ancient mum originating from north-east Africa and known as an ancient Egyptian Mummy.

If your mum is this kind of mummy, I've only got one thing to say to you: I hope you take after your dad!

Typical Mummy-Moan:

Have you been cleaning your bike chain in the kitchen sphinx again?

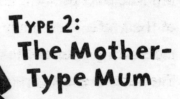

TYPE 2: The Mother-Type Mum

A mum who thinks she's the best thing since the Xbox was invented and who therefore likes to be called Mother or, more correctly, Mother Superior. If your mum looks like this, tell her to stop buying her clothes from the local convent's jumble sales.

Typical Mother–Superior Saying: Nun.

TYPE 3:
The Mama-Type Mum

Mums who are dead posh like to be called Mama (pronounced *Mar-Ma*), which is short for Mar-Ma-Ladies.

If your mum is one of these Mar-Ma-Ladies, she will be very easy to handle. Just keep her in the fridge and only bring her out at breakfast time.

THIN CUT

Typical Mar–Ma–lady Saying:

Use a spoon to get me out of the jar, not a knife!

The chances are that your mum is not an ancient Egyptian, or a nun, or a jar of marmalade, so learning how to handle her is going to be rather like conjuring, in other words, a very tricky business.

Fortunately, help is at hand from me — the Quizmister — the celebrated author of this very helpful book you are reading. For the first time in the history of mankind — and more importantly, of mumkind — an incredibly brilliant inventor* has built a giant super computer to provide answers to some of the most difficult problems people have with their mums. It's called MUMBO (stands for **MUM**s had **B**etter watch **O**ut) JUMBO.

Hi folks!

---

* This incredibly brilliant inventor is also incredibly modest and won't reveal his name. However, you can find out who he is by rearranging the following letters: E M.

Now, it's a well-known scientific fact that mums aren't like any other sort of people (just ask your dad). So first of all, I tried to discover what kind of mum I had. After spending a couple of minutes scouring the Internet, MUMBO JUMBO eventually flashed this message up on the screen:

Your mum
fell from
the sky.

I fell off my seat. I was stunned. (This was because I'd banged my head on the desk.)

"My mum fell from the sky?" I said.

"Are you sure?" I asked.

"Well, no. You are," I said. (I can't believe I'm talking to it...)

That's right, birdbrain. It's time for one of your quizzes...

I was beginning to wonder if building MUMBO JUMBO was a good idea, but he had a point. Actually he had four, one on each corner of his screen. Write your answers to this quiz on a piece of paper to prove your mum is an alien.

Quiz 1: Finding out your mum is an alien

1. Does your mum ever say any of the following to you, "I think you...

A: watch too much TV."

B: have far too much pocket money."

C: go to bed far too late."

2. "I think you don't...

A: get enough homework."

B: understand the meaning of tidiness."

C: eat enough cabbage."

3. Does your mum think it's OK
for you to wear any of the following?

A: a school blazer

B: an anorak

C: a hand-knitted pullover

4. Does your mum think
that any of the following people are cool?

A: Justin Bieber

B: Ant and Dec

C: The bloke who reads
The News at Ten

Snooze at Ten

WHAT YOUR SCORE MEANS:

If you've written an answer down for ANY
of the above questions, then ask yourself,

where on Earth has your mum been living for the past five years? To which the answer must be...nowhere on Earth. Therefore she must be an alien.

To which there is a very obvious question... "Which planet does she come from?"

To which there is a very obvious answer..."Ma(r)s."

"But how did she manage to get to Mars and back?" I hear you ask. (*Yes, I can hear you from where I am sitting.*)

To which there is, yet again, a very obvious answer.

"On her Mother ship!"

How To Handle Your Mum:

Stage Three

How mums get their superhu-mum powers

Once I'd discovered that my mum was an alien, a lot of things began to fall into place. Like why she calls my dad "Hunkikins" when she thinks I'm not listening, when really his name is Eric. ("Hunkikins" is obviously the alien translation of Eric.) But that still didn't explain just why mums are so difficult to handle. I asked MUMBO JUMBO to explain.

And MUMBO JUMBO said:

All mums have children.

"I could've told you that!" I said.

And MUMBO JUMBO replied:

I asked MUMBO JUMBO why having children made mums different.

And MUMBO JUMBO replied:

MUMBO JUMBO had obviously got a computer virus. So I put it to bed with a mug of hot honey and lemon and when it felt better it said this:

When they are going to have a baby, mums get cravings for strange mixtures of foods, such as Brussels sprouts with custard, or chocolate cake and cold gravy, or ice cream and  tomato sauce, or a hamburger... sorry... that's just too much. I feel sick.

I need to go back to bed. I'll see you in the next chapter...

ZZZZzzzzzz...

"Well, this is just great," I said. "What am I supposed to do now?"

ZZZZZZZZzzzzzzzzz...

So I made up another chapter to wake him up.

How To Handle Your Mum: Stage Three-and-a-half

I said, "Wake up!"

And MUMBO JUMBO said:

You said I could sleep until the next chapter.

I said "This is the next chapter."
And MUMBO JUMBO said:

So I said, "I think we'll have to call someone to get you de-bugged."

Then MUMBO JUMBO said:

"Bo, bon't borry. Ben dey are dohing to hab a bubby, bubs ged crabings for drange bixtures of foobs — dorry I've dill godda blogged up dose from dis virus!"

So I said, "Oh, blow it!"

And so MUMBO did.

PARP!

"Ooooooh! That's better! I was trying to say eating these strange mixtures of food gives mums certain superhu-mum powers. All mums have at least one of these superhu-mum powers. The most common of these superhu-mum powers is **Radar Ear**."

"Pardon? I didn't quite catch that—"

RADAR EAR!!!!

How To Handle Your Mum:

Stage Four

The five superhu-mum powers and how to combat them

1. Radar Ear

So what is Radar Ear exactly?

I clicked the mouse to see what information MUMBO JUMBO had on mums with Radar Ear. Very quickly it said:

Then it said:

And I suddenly realised what the problem was. MUMBO JUMBO was so scared of my mouse it had leapt up onto my bookcase and there it stayed. Luckily I've got a back-up computer with everything I know on it. It's called My Brain. So here is everything I know about mums with Radar Ear.

An ordinary ear looks like this:

A mum's Radar Ear looks like this:

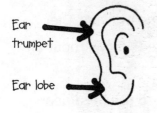

Ear trumpet

Ear lobe

Satellite dish

Ear stud concealing special microchip

The kind of things mums with Radar Ears tend to say are:

"I hear that the Queen's coming to open the new by-pass."

Now, did that mum actually go to Buckingham Palace and hear the Queen say: "Philip! Ay'm just orff to open the new Clogbury

baypass. Ay've left you a boil-in-the-bag
kipper for your supper."

Of course not. Rather, she was just about
to give the cat its dinner when she decided
to turn her Radar Ear in the approximate
direction of London SW1 and, so powerful
is a mum's Radar Ear, she heard what the
Queen was saying to Prince Philip without any
difficulty whatsoever.

When your mum comes to use her Radar
Ear on you, however, it works in a particularly
devilish way. It can actually decide what to
pick up and what not to. It picks up everything
you don't want your mum to hear, and it cuts
out anything you do want her to hear.

I asked MUMBO JUMBO to explain and
it said:

So I did. And MUMBO JUMBO came up with the following table:

I said, "That's a very old joke."
And MUMBO JUMBO replied:

It's a very old table.

Then MUMBO JUMBO came up with this table on the next page:

Words and phrases of yours that a mum's Radar Ear always picks up	Words and phrases of yours that a mum's Radar Ear never picks up
"!$!*$!!" (that is, any word that is at all rude.)	"I'd like (a) a 20-gear mountain bike, (b) a horse and stables for the back garden for my birthday, please."
"No, of course my mum won't mind if we look after your pet tarantula for the holidays."	"Can we go to Disneyland for our holiday this year?"
"Chomp, chomp!" (tucking into the chocolate gateau that's thawing specially for your mum to take to the school Parent's Association dance.)	"Can Karen and I go to the One Direction concert, please?"

You can work out how good your mum's Radar Ear is by conducting the following experiment:

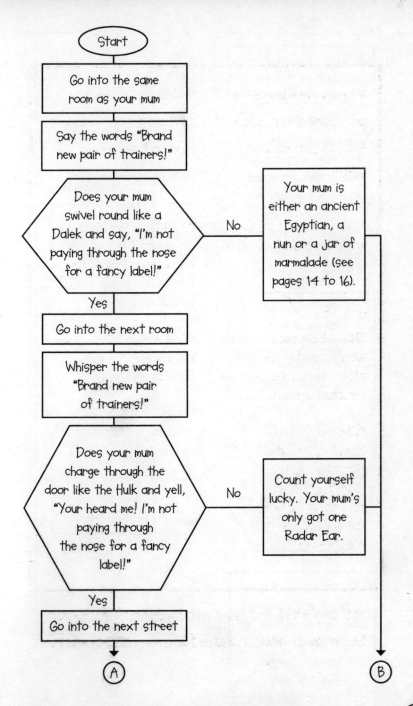

Start

Go into the same room as your mum

Say the words "Brand new pair of trainers!"

Does your mum swivel round like a Dalek and say, "I'm not paying through the nose for a fancy label!" — No → Your mum is either an ancient Egyptian, a nun or a jar of marmalade (see pages 14 to 16).

Yes

Go into the next room

Whisper the words "Brand new pair of trainers!"

Does your mum charge through the door like the Hulk and yell, "Your heard me! I'm not paying through the nose for a fancy label!" — No → Count yourself lucky. Your mum's only got one Radar Ear.

Yes

Go into the next street

A

B

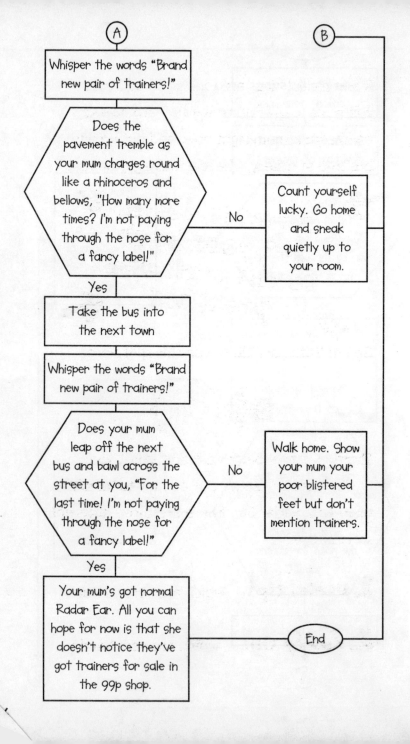

If you think things are looking so bad that you want to give up trying to learn how to handle your mum right now, and put up with a lifetime of misery, I have a message for you.

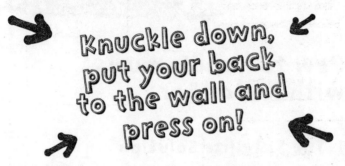

Knuckle down, put your back to the wall and press on!

Go on! With your thumb on this spot here:

There! You feel better already, don't you?

Now here are some tips on how to handle a mum with Radar Ear. There are three different sorts of tips:

1. Useful tips — which are very useful

2. Handy tips — which are very handy

3. Rubbish tips — which are where the non-recyclable rubbish in your bins is taken to.

How to handle mums with Radar Ear

1. The Satellite Solution

Give your mum and her Radar Ear something

else to listen to other than you. The most obvious thing to do is to strap her to the chimney, so that her Radar Ear can operate as a satellite dish. I say this is obvious, because if your mum is strapped to the chimney, she certainly will be (obvious, that is).

Advantage of this solution: the rest of your family will be really pleased with you, because they'll be able to watch Premiership football on Monday nights.

Disadvantage of this solution: with your mum strapped to the chimney, you'll have to get your own tea.

2. The Ear Muff Method

Knit your mum a pair of really thick woolly ear muffs. She'll be so touched by your thoughtfulness that she'll wear them all the time you're around.

Advantage of this method: you won't have to get your own tea.

Disadvantage of this method: have you ever tried knitting a pair of ear muffs?

3. The Semaphore Solution

Instead of talking, you could use semaphore. This is a system of communication that uses

flags, so it is completely silent and can never be picked up by Radar Ear or any other sort of ear for that matter.

Advantage of this solution: you could earn extra pocket money by hiring yourself out to local fêtes as a flag pole.

Disadvantage of this solution: limited as a means of communication — have you ever tried doing semaphore while riding a bike or cleaning your teeth, for example?

2. Gamma-Ray Eye

What is Gamma-Ray Eye?

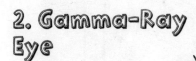

Are you asking me?

"If I am, are you going to tell me the answer?" I replied.

MUMBO JUMBO said:

Yes, if I can have something to eat.

So I gave it a computer chip sandwich.

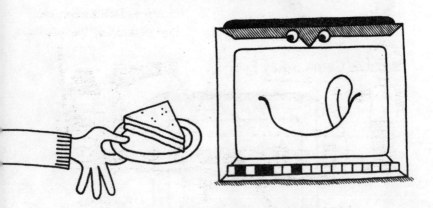

It took a couple of megabytes and said:

Gamma–Ray Eye enables your mum to actually see through things. For example, to anyone else your bed looks like this:

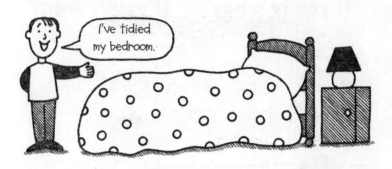

But to a mum with Gamma–Ray Eye, it looks like this:

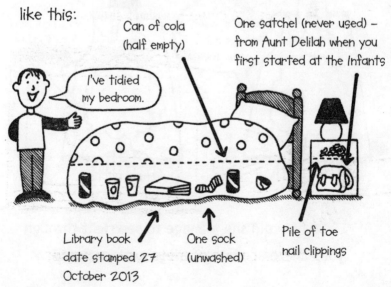

Can of cola (half empty)

One satchel (never used) – from Aunt Delilah when you first started at the Infants

Library book date stamped 27 October 2013

One sock (unwashed)

Pile of toe nail clippings

Another problem comes when you're leaving the house. You're halfway to the front door with your back to your mum, but she calls out:

If you're a boy   **If you're a girl**

So how did she manage to see right through you? There are two possible explanations:

1. Either, like the Invisible Man, you are made up of completely see-through matter;

2. Or your mum's got Gamma-Ray Eye.

How to handle mums with Gamma-Ray Eye

"Eh?!"

At first I thought MUMBO JUMBO had suddenly learnt to speak Russian, then I realised this tip on how to deal with Gamma Ray Eye was so secret, MUMBO JUMBO would only reveal the details in code. What I needed was a code breaker.

So I Googled *Code Breakers* and found Rob Deeke Cars, which is a code for Code Breakers. I phoned them and they told me there were three methods of breaking MUMBO JUMBO's code:

1. A stupid way

Hit it hard with a hammer.

2. A hard way

Read it from right to left.

3. An easy way

Place a mirror along the left-hand side of the page.

OK, readers. Choose your method and break MUMBO JUMBO's code.

> **Handling Gamma-Ray Eye**
> If there's anything you don't want your mum to see make sure you are holding a mirror up in front of her face.

What happens, of course, is that the Gamma-Rays are directed straight back at your mum. Elpmis, isn't it?

3. Laser Blaster Tongue

What is Laser Blaster Tongue?

Sharp, cutting and deadly — that's what a mum's Laser Blaster Tongue is. It enables them to come out with really devastating comments. Here are some examples:

(When you've tried to clean your bike by putting it in the dishwasher):

"You've got as much brain as a bowl of baked beans."

(When you've asked for the 100th time if you can have a pony for your birthday):

"Why on earth do we need a pony when we've already got a donkey?"

(She means you.)

(When you've just put on your brand new party anthems compilation):

"Oh, no! Sounds like the cat's got trapped in the tumble dryer again!"

Laser Blaster Tongue works like a missile targeting system. Your mum will pick a target then deliver a suitable laser-tongued phrase to blast you away. See if you select the right Laser Blaster Tongue response to these targets.

Common targets of mums' Laser Tongues	Common phrases of mums' Laser Tongues
Your incredible brain power	about as much use as a chocolate hammer
Your exquisite table manners	two gherkins short of a Big Mac
Your favourite actor/singer	as much taste as a second-hand herbal tea bag
Your superb taste in TV programmes	picked up in the Safari Park
Your keen clothes sense	looks like a herd of wildebeest have just stormed through it
The state of your room	makes a sack of spuds look chic
Your amazing ability to stand on your head for seven and a half minutes without being sick	like Frankenstein's monster, but without his charm

How to handle mums with Laser Blaster Tongue

MUMBO JUMBO said:

And I said, "Any more talk like that, and I'll start using that mouse again!"

So MUMBO JUMBO said:

I said, "Thank you very much."

Then I realised that this was MUMBO JUMBO's handy hint on how to handle your mum's Laser Blaster Tongue. (i.e. be like Ken* and creep.)

This is how it works:

MUM: Why on earth do we need a pony when we've got a donkey? (See above.)

YOU: Oh, Mum! Why on earth do we need a pony when we've got a donkey! Oh, how clever...! How witty—

MUM: Do you really think so?

YOU: Oh, yes. Ha, ha, ha! Ho, ho, ho!

MUM: It was rather good, now you come to mention it. Ho, ho, ho!

YOU: Ha, ha, ha! I wish I could be as witty as that!

* Full name: Ken-I-do-that-for-you-miss-please-miss, aka the teacher's pet.

MUM: I bet you do! Ho, ho, ho!

YOU: Ha, ha, ha! You are going to let me have a pony, aren't you, Mum? You're so clever, Mum!

MUM: Yes, of course I am, dear!

YOU: Thank you very much, Mum!

4. Robo Leg

What is Robo Leg?

Compared with a mum's speed as she catches you sneaking out for a game of football without having first tidied your room, Usain Bolt is about as fast as a snail with a zimmer frame. Compared with a mum's speed as she catches you sneaking up to your room without first having put your dirty dinner plates in the sink, Jessica Ennis-Hill is about as fast as a tortoise with bricks in its boots.

Yes, Superhu-mums are fast!

The really clever thing, though, is that they don't look fast. That's why it's so easy to be taken by surprise. It's all to do with clothes.

On top your
mum might look
like this:

But underneath,
she'll be wearing
something like this:

In fact, in your mum's eyes, your house is
nothing more than an athletics stadium.

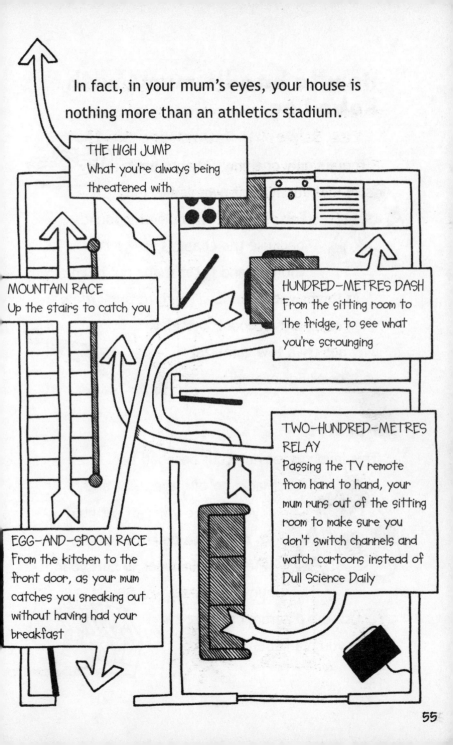

THE HIGH JUMP
What you're always being
threatened with

MOUNTAIN RACE
Up the stairs to catch you

HUNDRED-METRES DASH
From the sitting room to
the fridge, to see what
you're scrounging

TWO-HUNDRED-METRES
RELAY
Passing the TV remote
from hand to hand, your
mum runs out of the sitting
room to make sure you
don't switch channels and
watch cartoons instead of
Dull Science Daily

EGG-AND-SPOON RACE
From the kitchen to the
front door, as your mum
catches you sneaking out
without having had your
breakfast

How to handle mums with Robo Leg

There's only one way — try to beat them at their own game.

This is not as difficult as it sounds, because the chances are you're younger and fitter than your mum.

As mums with Robo Leg seem to think life's one continuous school sports day, why not try a few games of your own? For example:

Hurdles

This involves leaving your baseball bat, rucksack, gerbil cage, bike and anything else you can get hold of in various places throughout the house in order to halt your mum's progress.

Use the diagram opposite to help you plan your strategy.

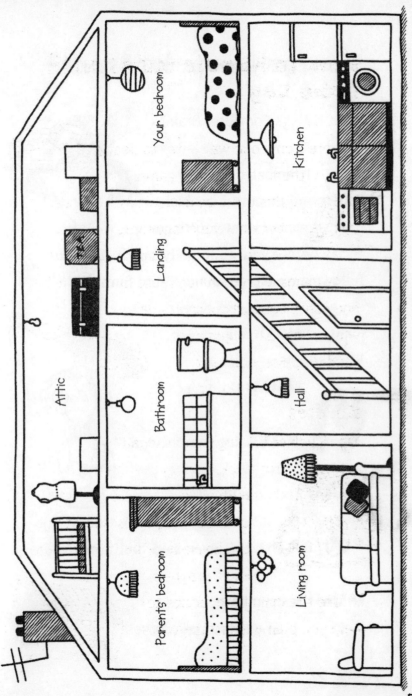

Your bedroom

Kitchen

Landing

Bathroom

Attic

Hall

Parents' bedroom

Living room

57

5. Mega Computer Brain

What is Mega Computer Brain?

This truly amazing
Superhu-mum power enables
mums to know what you're going
to say before you've actually said it. Does the
following exchange sound all too familiar?

YOU: Mum...

MUM: No, you can't.

YOU: Just this once...?

MUM: And no buts.

YOU: But I haven't even said "but" yet!

MUM: Yes you have.

(She's right, of course!)

MUM: Twice. Anyway, why do you want to...
(insert whatever it is you were going to ask
her for).

(See! she knows – without you asking!)

YOU: Oh, go on, Mum! Please! If you let
me, I'll—

(You're about to say, "I'll take the dog for a
walk for you," when your mum butts in.)

MUM: Dad took it through the car wash
yesterday.

(Yahoo! Jubilation! You've got her this time, you think! Her Mega Computer Brain has failed her! She thinks you were going to offer to wash the car, rather than take the dog for a walk!)

YOU: Dad took our dog Rover through the car wash?

MUM: No, Dad took our car Rover through the car wash.

YOU: I wasn't going to offer to wash the car, Mum. I was going to offer to take our dog for a walk. That surprised you, didn't it? Eh?

MUM: It certainly did. We haven't got
a dog!
(You are about to crawl up to your room,
totally and utterly defeated in your request,
when your mum strikes the killer blow.)

MUM: OK!

YOU: OK what, Mum?

MUM: You've been very good
about the house lately, so I'll let you
— just this once. Now run along.

(At this point you realise with a sickening
feeling that, what with all the argy-bargying
with your mum, you've completely
forgotten what it was you'd
asked her for in the first place!
So you continue crawling up
to your room, totally and
utterly defeated.)

How to handle mums with Mega Computer Brain

I asked MUMBO JUMBO for advice on this most tricky of all the Superhu-mum powers and it said:

Pass

Which is another way of saying, write the following letter:

Dear Mr Humphrys,

Please could you enter my mum for this year's BBC Mastermind competition. Her chosen subject will be Major Battles of the School Holidays – July to September.

Yours sincerely (insert your name)

Once entered as a "Mastermind" contestant, your mum will have to start learning to answer questions after she has heard them and not before.

Trace over this "Mum" outline and label any other powers you think you own mum has:

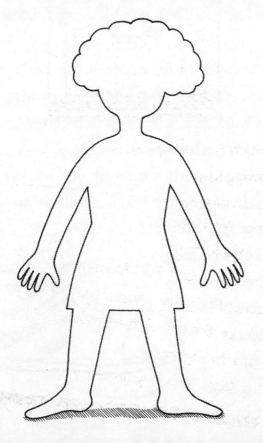

How To Handle Your Mum:

Stage Five:

Training your mum

1. The Training Program

Now that you've learnt about Superhu-mum powers and have practised dealing with them, you should be in a position to progress to Stage Five — training your mum.

To undertake this training, you will need the help of a decent trainer. Trainers are very flash people with fat, soft bottoms and they have given their name to a particular type of running shoe.

However, when I asked the top trainer in the country for his advice on the Training of Mums, he sent me a very cross email. It was:

Then he sent me another very cross email:

Dear Quizmister,
   I am not going to give you any help on the Training of Mums because you have been very rude about my bottom.
   Yours sincerely,
   A. Boot

As you probably know, there is only one thing to do if you can't get hold of a decent trainer, and that is to get hold of a decent pair of Flash USBs (Ultra Super Boots).

However, because of a misunderstanding in the shop, I didn't end up with a pair of Flash Ultra Super Boots. I got a Flash USB instead.

So I connected it to MUMBO JUMBO.

And MUMBO JUMBO said:

Obviously, the training of mums is a ticklish subject. Then it said:

THE TRAINING PROGRAM:
QUIZ 2: (Hang on a minute, I thought I was the only one setting quizzes!)

1. Is your mum older than you? **YES/NO**

2. Is your mum a woman? **YES/NO**
If your answered YES to 1 and 2, proceed to 3:*

3. Does your mum expect you to go to bed

    A: before the *Ten O'clock News*

    B: after the *Ten O'clock News*

    C: before *Coronation Street*?

4. During school holidays, does your mum let you stay in bed until

    A: sunrise

    B: lunchtime

    C: sunset?

5. You're off school sick. You ask your mum if you can watch TV. What is her reply?

    A: If you're too ill to go to school, you're too ill to watch telly.

    B: Yes, but only those educational DVDs your nan bought for Christmas.

    C: Yes, but only quiz shows.

* If your answer to either Question 1 or Question 2 is NO, then contact one of the Sunday newspapers immediately and offer to sell them your story for a huge sum of money.

6. You ask your mum if you can start a football club, using your back garden as your home ground. What does she say next?

A: And what about the greenhouse windows?

B: Only if you appoint me as manager.

C: Yes, of course you can.

HOW TO SCORE:

3A: One point.

3B: Another point.

3C: Lucky you — have you ever seen *Coronation Street*? It's a lot less interesting than being asleep in bed.

4A: One point.

4B: Another point.

4C: Your mum thinks you're a vampire. Pretty soon she'll be hanging garlic from your bedroom door.

5A: Minus twelve points.

5B: No point at all, really.

5C: Your mum thinks your illness has gone to your brain.

6A: Minus ten points (and minus ten windows).

6B: Half a point. At least if she's the manager she won't be able to be the ref.

6C: You obviously haven't got a back garden.

WHAT YOUR SCORE MEANS:

Score:

Over three – see your teacher about taking extra maths.

Under three — join the club. You have got a mum who is unreasonable.

2. Training Your Mum to Stop Being Nosey

When I came to look at the posts
on my blog on this subject,
I found these:

Oh, all right!
There were lots
of comments too, every one of which had
been opened by my mum. She's got parental
controls turned on. Here is one of the posts:

Dear Uncle Aggie,
I need to turn my bedroom into a car
workshop, so that me and my mates
can get our motor ready for the
championships, but my mum is very
nosey and I'm afraid she'll see.
    What shall I do?
    Yours, Hewis Lamilton

I fed this letter into MUMBO JUMBO and it replied:

And I said, "Of course it's not! It's an online name I use to write my Quizmister blog."

"Yes... You're building up to a joke here, aren't you?"

"I knew it."

You taught me everything I know.

"So, I should have expected your jokes to be as bad as mine."

Well, I still have a lot of free memory.

"Just let me do the jokes. Time to respond to Hewis Lamilton."

Dear Hewis Lamilton,
Here's what you should do to train
your mum to stop being nosey —
use a red herring. You can get these
at the fishmonger for about £5.00
per kilogram.
    Yours, Uncle Aggie

So that was that one solved! Then I looked
at the next post. It read:

Dear Uncle Aggie,
The red herring idea
was no use. My mum's
a vegetarian.
    Yours,
    Hewis Lamilton

So, I replied:

Dear Hewis Lamilton,

Make your own red herring using a toilet roll tube and an old coat hanger. Then say to your mum, "No! No! Please don't look in my room!" She will naturally think you've got something to hide. She storms in – and sees the red herring. "Ooh, you're getting on with a science project," she says. "I thought for one nasty moment you were trying to conceal a car workshop in here!" She won't bother being nosey for at least a week – time enough for you to set up a car workshop in your room.

Yours,

Uncle Aggie

P.S. Alternatively you could just pack up Formula One racing instead.

3. Training Your Mum to be Reasonable

There is a very popular saying amongst mums:

"Oh, for goodness' sake, (insert name here)! Be reasonable!"

And of course, you are — all the time. Unfortunately, training mums to be reasonable can be very difficult indeed. It involves going Over The Top or, as it is more commonly known, "going O.T.T." Here are a couple of typical case histories.

Case History Number One

The history of this case is that it was made in 1984 by a Mr Reginald Arkwright of Northampton, and after an utterly uneventful life, it has turned up as an illustration in this book.

Case History Number Two

Mo Rapping wants to go and buy the new album by her favourite group, Wrong Direction. Her mum, though, thinks the only singer suitable for a ten-year-old girl to listen to is Gary Barlow. So Mo goes O.T.T. and pretends she's into heavy metal...

MO: Mum, can I go to the Squidgy Bogies concert?

MUM: (Shaking with terror) For goodness' sake, Mo! Be reasonable! They're Heavy Mental!

MO: Heavy metal — that's right, Mum. They really blow your brains out.

MUM: (Terrified that her darling daughter is about to become a heavy metal groupie) Oh dear, oh dear! What's wrong with decent music?

MO: What do you mean, "decent music"?

MUM: Well ... er ... not heavy metal, for a start!

MO: Something quieter?

MUM: Yes...

MO: Like Wrong Direction, do you mean?

MUM: (sighs) Look, if I let you get the Wrong Direction album, will you promise not to mention the Squidgy Bogies again?

MO: Of course, Mum.

See? Easy, isn't it?

4. Training Your Mum not to Embarrass You in Public

It's as natural (and as unpleasant) as goat's yoghurt for your mum to embarrass you in public.

When I asked MUMBO JUMBO why this should be so, it said:

Mums embarrassing their sons and daughters in public? It's all part of their make-up.

But I shouldn't advise you to go hunting through your mum's make-up bag to find it. Because what with her Gamma-Ray Eye and Mega Computer Brain, she's bound to catch you. If you're a girl this could be very awkward, and if you're a boy it could be awkward, embarrassing, totally humiliating and an utter disaster.

The most common way for people to avoid being embarrassed by their mums in public is to hide.

Hiding your face

Ever wondered why bank robbers wear stocking masks? It's nothing to do with them not wanting to be seen by the security cameras, it's simply that they got fed up with their mums coming up to them in the banks they were robbing and saying things like:

"Ronnie! Get back home immediately and finish your breakfast. I've made bread-and-butter soldiers for you, specially."

Just hiding...

Try walking six paces behind your mum, when you're out with her. Then when she says to Mrs Noggin from five doors down: "Doesn't he take after his Aunt Vera?" you can duck behind the nearest wheeliebin and Mrs Noggin will assume your mum is referring to a passing Rottweiler.

safe distance

However, hiding won't do anything to cure the problem. You've got to train your mum to stop embarrassing you in public, and the only way to do this is to use a Secret Agent...

How To Handle Your Mum:

Stage Six

Using a Secret Agent

The Secret Agents you use to help you handle your mum are so-called because you keep it a secret from them that they are working for you.

There are three types of Secret Agent who are worth seeking out to help you with your work:

1. grannies

2. ghouls

3. gerbils

Grannies

The best sort of granny to have as a Secret Agent is the sort who is your mum's mum. They remember (usually only too well) just what your mum was like when she was your age.*

This, as we will see later, can be very useful indeed.

You may already know of the exploits of the most famous Granny Secret Agent of them all. If you do, it can mean only one thing — you've read this book before...

Granny Bond 0070

Licensed to knit

Granny Bond sat in her armchair watching snooker on the telly. There was a knock at

---

* Yes, incredible though it may seem, your mum was once a fun-loving, sensitive, totally reasonable young person like yourself!

the door. In walked her granddaughter, Brooke Bond.

"Oh, Granny Bond, you've got to help me to handle my mum!"

"Let's just call her M, shall we?" said Granny Bond. "Is she being embarrassing in public again?"

"You bet!" said Brooke.

"What's she done this time?"

"It's not what she's done, it's what she wears! Fluorescent purple and orange leggings, an old baggy sweater and beads in her hair."

"Ah! Your mum thinks she's being cool," explained Granny Bond.

"Cool! I should think she's freezing!" said Brooke.

"Ssshhh!" said Granny Bond. "Here comes your mum now!"

In came Brooke's mum, dressed in her fluorescent purple and orange leggings, baggy sweater and beads.

"Georgina!" said Granny Bond. "You are not going out looking like that!"

"But, Mum!" said Brooke's mum.

"Go upstairs and change," said Granny Bond. "You've got as much taste as a second-hand herbal tea bag!"

"That phrase sounds familiar," said Brooke.

"It should do," replied Granny Bond. "It's on page 50 of this very book!"

And thanks to Secret Agent Granny Bond, Brooke's mum never ever embarrassed her in public again by wearing her purple and orange leggings, her old sweater and beads.

Ghouls

The best kind of ghouls to use as Secret Agents
are those who blow gum in old ladies' faces,
swear, spit, spray Darren 4 Karen on lamp
posts, pass wind during school assembly and
generally behave very badly indeed. There is
probably at least one in your class.

Boy ghoul   Girl ghoul

Now, you may think "I'd rather suffer years
of torture at the hands of my mum, than have
to talk to the likes of Lenny Lickspittle or
Felicity Foulmouth," but the beauty of using a
ghoul as a Secret Agent is that you don't have
to talk to them at all!

The way it works is like this: your mum absolutely hates this sort of ghoul. When she mentions such people her voice takes on a tone that makes Lord Snooty sound like somebody out of *EastEnders*.

"You don't sit next to Lenny Lickspittle in class, surely?"

"Come away from the front window! That Felicity Foulmouth is passing the house."

Your mum is absolutely terrified that you will end up as the next Lenny Lickspittle or Felicity Foulmouth! So here's an example of how to use a ghoul as a Secret Agent:

(Scene: your local department store. Your mum is buying you a new coat. Her eyes fall upon a dreadful anorak thing that looks as if it was last worn by Postman Pat's granny. But there's no doubt about it – your mum thinks it's just the thing for a girl like you.)

MUM: It certainly looks as if it will last.

(You have visions of this anorak still not being worn out by the time you leave school. Meanwhile, you have your eyes on a rather natty zip-up jacket. Time to use your Secret Agent.)

YOU: Oh, Mum! You wouldn't make me wear that anorak?

MUM: And why not? I suppose it isn't "cool", is that it?

YOU: No, it's definitely not "cool", as you put it.

MUM: Huh!

YOU: And the reason it's not "cool" is that it's just the sort of coat Felicity Foulmouth would wear!

MUM: (horrified) Is it?

YOU: Definitely!

MUM: Oh, dear!

YOU: I don't want to go around looking like Felicity Foulmouth, do I?

MUM: (with feeling) Er, no... You most certainly do not.

(Steer your mum in the direction of the natty zip-up jacket.)

Gerbils

All schools have
a pet gerbil.
These harmless
little creatures sit
around all day without
much to do, so you
might as well employ them as Secret Agents.
They can be used in a similar way to ghouls.

Your mum probably doesn't hate the school
gerbil in the same way as she hates Felicity
Foulmouth and Lenny Lickspittle, but she's
terrified of having the poor little thing in the
house. She's afraid that it will escape, or
even expire while it's under your roof. If that
happened, of course, she would die of shame
because the neighbours would all avoid her
in the street and the RSPCA would set up an
undercover round-the-clock watch on your
house. So here's an example of how to use the
school gerbil as a Secret Agent in the battle to
handle your mum:

(Scene: the kitchen. The problem: your best mate Steve has invited you to go with him and stay at his cousin's for a weekend. His cousin lives a few miles from Alton Towers!)

MUM: (showing typical superhu—mum powers) No, you can't go away for the weekend.

YOU: But, Mum! Steve's invited me. Wouldn't it be rude to say no?

MUM: It's the Community Association car boot sale on Sunday. I was relying on you to give me a hand.

(Yee—oww!!! This is even more serious than you thought! You'd forgotten about the dreaded Community Association car boot sale. Time to call in your Secret Agent.)

YOU: (sigh) Oh, well. I suppose Old Soggy* will be pleased.

MUM: Why should Mrs Sponge** be pleased?

YOU: It means we'll be able to have the class gerbil for the weekend after all.

MUM: (White with fear) What? Eh? Er, no... Yes, of course you can go with Steve to his cousin's for the weekend!

(Time to go upstairs and start packing your rucksack.)

R.I.P.

* Your class teacher's nickname.
** Your class teacher's real name.

How To Handle Your Mum:

Stage Seven

The Mum-handling Test

Test your knowledge of mums and how
to handle them in MY special final quiz
(I'm doing them again, not MUMBO JUMBO).

1. Which of these are superhu-mum powers?

A: Runny Nose

B: Pain in the Neck

C: Gamma-Ray Eye

D: False Teeth

E: Laser Blaster Tongue

F: Mega Computer Brain

2. Which of these will help you train your mum?

A: A packet of dog biscuits

B: A flock of sheep

C: A Secret Agent

3. Who would cause you most embarrassment in your local shopping mall?

A: Your dog peeing on the floor

B: Your mum

C: Peppa Pig

4. Your mum tells you your room is a mess and starts fuming. Do you

A: ring the fire brigade?

B: buy a mirror?

C: tidy it up?

5. Which of these is a rare type of mum?

A: A Su-mum-tran Orangutan

B: A Thingamummy

C: A jar of marmalade

6. Where do computers believe mums are from?

A: Handbags

B: Ma(r)s

C: Asda

7. Why did the chicken cross the road?

  A: To get to the other side.

  B: Because it was egged on.

  C: To avoid being embarrassed
by its mum in public.

8. Which of the following things should
you never say to your mum?

  A: "What did you do in the war?"

  B: "Granny has that dress."

  C: "Your home-made burgers are
  almost as good as McDonald's."

9. How old is your mum likely to wish you were?

  A: Old enough to know better

  B: Old enough to buy a car

  C: Two and a half

10. On what occasion do your mum and your
friends' mums all get together for a chat?

  A: A coffee morning

  B: A hen party

  C: Your birthday party

Answers

1: 1 point each for C; E; F. Half a point for E (False teeth). This is a Superhu-gum power.

2: 1 point for C. 1 point for B (providing your mum is Little, her first name is Bo and your surname is Peep).

3: 1 point for B.

4: 2 points for B and 999 for the fire brigade.

5: 2 points for C and a 1,000 whatsitsnames for thingamummy.

6: 2 points for B. If you put A, then I'd like to know just what you were doing looking in your mum's handbag.

7: 1 point for C. Nothing whatsoever for B – it's one of the very worst jokes I have ever heard.

8: None of them! Take away a hundred points for each thing you thought you could say to your mum.

9: Deduct 50 points for B. Score 1 point for A (every mum says this at least once a day). Score 2 points for C. All mums like to think they're a lot younger than they are, which they would be if you were still two and a half!

10: They might call it A or B, but of course it's C. Score 2 for C.

WHAT YOUR SCORE MEANS:

Minus 1,050 or more? Time to put some more batteries in your calculator.

Between minus 1,050 and 107. OK, you know the theory, now go out and practise it!

Between 10 and 19? Glad I'm not your mum!

More than 19½? You can't count.

978 1 4451 2394 3 pb   978 1 4451 2398 1 ebook

School can drive you bonkers.
School can be desperately dull
...but you **have** to go to school
(it's the law!)

Like most schools, yours is probably stuffed with troublesome
teachers and potty pupils. And like most kids, you probably
think you'll never survive until the end of term...
That's where you're soooo wrong.

How to Handle Your School is here to
"help" with all your school-related pains in the...neck.